SCOT RITCHIE'S
GHOULIEST EVER
PUZZLE BOOK

LITTLE HARE
www.littleharebooks.com

Little Hare Books
8/21 Mary Street, Surry Hills
NSW 2010 AUSTRALIA

www.littleharebooks.com

First published in 2008

National Library of Australia
Cataloguing-in-Publication entry:

Ritchie, Scot.

Scot Ritchie's ghouliest ever puzzle book / Scot Ritchie

978 1 921272 62 2 (pbk.)

For primary school age.

Ghosts--Juvenile literature
Picture puzzles--Juvenile literature.
Maze puzzles--Juvenile literature.

793.73

Designed by Simon Rattray
Produced in Singapore by Pica Digital Ltd
Printed in China at Everbest Printing

5 4 3 2 1

WHAT'S THAT BUMP? WHAT'S THAT SQUEAK?

Do you LOVE being scared by strange noises in the night or getting goose bumps from stories of haunted houses?

If you do, you're in the right place!

Welcome to my friend Scot Ritchie's Ghouliest Ever Puzzle Book. It's the place where you can get those scary goose bumps and test your brainpower at the same time!

Have you ever been to a zombie playground or searched an ancient pyramid for the pharaoh's treasure? Inside this book we'll do both these things! We'll also visit a deserted graveyard (my favourite!), a house haunted by poltergeists and even a bloodcurdling bogeyman beach party. It's going to be scary, but lots of fun too, because there are tons of games, mazes and puzzles along the way.

Well, what are you waiting for? Get out your torch (and put the ghostcatcher on speed dial) because here we go!

For even more fun see if you can find me (Skout the Skeleton Dog) in every scene.

Don't look now, but if you want to find the answers, or more information about the Freaky Facts on every page, check the back of the book.

Happy haunting,

Skout

THE DAY OF THE DEAD

The Day of the Dead is a celebration and skeleton lady Catrína and her friends have been doing some *bone-rattling* baking!

Which tray has exactly the same cookies as the ones on the tray that Catrína is delivering? Which has the most cookies?

HOUSE ON THE HILL

This spooky house is haunted. A ghost has passed through and caused some trouble.

Can you find 25 things that have changed between the pictures?

There are some ghostly mice running all around this house. Can you find 2 mice with something unusual about them?

FREAKY FACTS

There is a way to get rid of the ghosts in your attic once and for all.

Check the back of the book to find out how.

AROUND THE C-C-CAMPFIRE

Camping in the backyard *seems* safe – you're only one scream away from the house! But look in those dark bushes ...

How many creepy faces can you see? Can you spot the 4 that are different from the rest?

FREAKY FACTS

Some people panic when they imagine ghosts are around. But you might be surprised where the word 'panic' comes from ...

Check the back of the book to find out.

GHOULS AND GOBLINS

Ghouls and goblins live in graveyards, caves and other dark, damp places.

Can you see 20 things that have been stolen or moved by the naughty goblins and ghastly ghouls?

FREAKY FACTS

Some people believe old houses have poltergeists because doors keep swinging open and banging shut all by themselves. But there could be a scientific explanation.

TRIP TO THE CEMETERY

These kids can't find their way from the gruesome tomb to the cemetery exit.

Can you help them? Take care not to fall into one of the open graves!

Can you spot 13 skeletons who have escaped and hidden around the cemetery? How many pirate skeletons are there?

FREAKY FACTS

Paris is famous for its beautiful old cemeteries and underground burial tunnels called catacombs. But before they were built, it was a different story.

HAUNTED CASTLE

This castle has a horrible history and these mirrors saw it all.

There are 17 differences between the reflections in the two mirrors.
Can you spot them?

One of these portraits is not identical. Can you tell which one?

GHOSTCATCHERS

The boy in the bottom corner needs to get to the ghostcatcher fast! Help him find his way through the maze.

Watch out for the 10 spooky ghosts as you go. Can you spot all 10? One ghost has lost his glasses – can you find them?

BOGEYMAN BEACH

Sometimes even the hardest-working
bogeyman needs a holiday.

Can you spot 2 things that the bogeymen
all have in common?

4 of these bogeymen have bogey pets.
Can you match the pets to the owners?

One bogeyman has a twin brother
who has fallen to pieces.
Can you put all the pieces back
together and see which bogeyman
the twin matches?

GHOST TOWN

These cowboys and cowgirls have come back to haunt their old town, even though it's deserted.

Can you find your way through this ghost town?

The cowboys wearing yellow scarves drink at the Horse Shine Hotel. Those wearing green scarves hang out at the Sarsaparilla Saloon. How many cowboys drink at the Horse Shine Hotel? How many go to the Sarsaparilla Saloon?

HORSE SHINE

EXIT

ENTER

Gunther's General Store

Sarsaparilla Saloon

Can you find Bloody Bradley, the ghouliest, ghostliest gunslinger of them all? He is wearing a cowboy hat, a red bandanna, a vest and no spurs.

FREAKY FACTS

When the wind blows, it might seem like ghosts are haunting these old towns. But the real reason they are deserted has nothing to do with ghosts.

THE DAY OF THE DEAD

During the Day of the Dead celebrations, people make offerings to departed loved ones and ancestors. These include flowers, toys, drinks, and treats such as sugar skulls and candied pumpkin. Many countries aside from Mexico hold Day of the Dead celebrations also.

HOUSE ON THE HILL

This Irish remedy removes ghosts from your house. At bedtime, toss dried peas on the floor. The ghosts will try to count the peas. However, ghosts are not good at this, so they'll lose count and have to keep starting again. After a few nights they'll become confused and leave.

HELP, MUMMY!

Many pyramids carry inscriptions with warnings to keep away. But, curses aside, deadly moulds can grow in tombs that are sealed shut, causing visitors to get sick. Either way, 8 of the 58 people who were present at the opening of Tutankhamen's tomb died within 12 years.

AROUND THE C-C-CAMPFIRE

The word 'panic' comes from Pan, the Greek god of the woods and fields. He was believed to be the source of strange sounds and other phenomena that could cause people to become disorientated, fearful and confused.

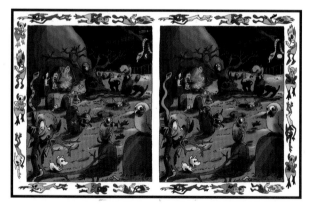

GHOULS AND GOBLINS

According to legend, ghouls live in graveyards and can change shape to trick unwary travellers into following them to deserted places! Goblins are said to dwell for short spells in mossy cracks in rocks and tree roots. Legends about goblins originated in Northern Europe.

SHAKE, RATTLE, ROLL

When the seasons change, an old house will settle and shift, causing wood to expand and contract. Doors can swing open or floorboards crack. At night, these noises seem loud and might sound like someone throwing things around.

TRIP TO THE CEMETERY

200-odd years ago, cemeteries in Paris became so crowded they couldn't take any more burials! Several new cemeteries were built on the outskirts of town. In 1786 all the remains from Cimetière des Innocents were moved to tunnels under Paris know as the Catacombs.

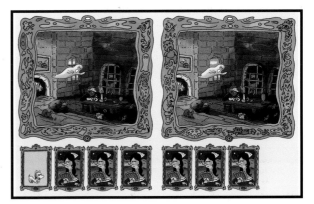

HAUNTED CASTLE

In many cultures the mirror is seen as a portal to the other side, where spirits live. Mirrors are covered during funerals to make sure nothing or nobody slips over to the living world — and the other way around!

GHOSTCATCHERS

Many people believe that ghosts haunt a particular spot because they want to pass on a message or to be around people and places they knew. They also believe that once ghosts have been acknowledged by the living, they will move on to the 'other side'.

BOGEYMAN BEACH

Nobody seems to know for sure where the English word 'bogeyman' comes from, but it was first used in 1836, and it meant 'the devil'. Earlier words like 'bogle' or 'bogy' date back to the 1500s, and meant 'frightening creature'.

ZOMBIE PLAYGROUND

Another name for 'zombie' is 'the undead'. This refers to beings that have died but don't know it yet. They act as if they are still alive. In reality there are no such beings, even though most cultures have some reference to them.

GHOST TOWN

A ghost town is a once-thriving town which has become deserted. There are many reasons why this can happen. Often, an area runs out of a precious material such as gold to mine or water to drink, and the people have to move to another place to make a living.

SOLUTIONS...

THE DAY OF THE DEAD

The tray circled in green has matching cookies. The tray circled in blue has the most cookies (13). The flowers circled in red are both missing a leaf.

HELP, MUMMY!

The microwave, computer and roller skates circled in green were not invented in Ancient Egypt.

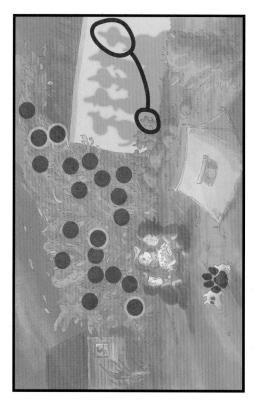

HOUSE ON THE HILL

The mouse circled in red has no tuft of hair on its forehead. The mouse circled in blue has no front leg.

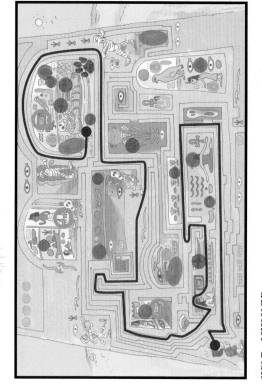

AROUND THE C-C-CAMPFIRE

There are 20 faces in the leaves. 4 faces only have one eye. The rat shadow circled in red is missing its right arm.

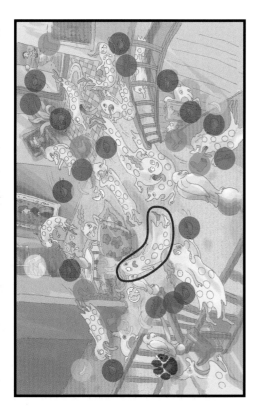

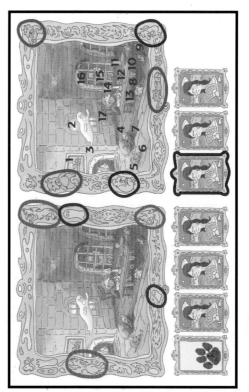

SHAKE, RATTLE, ROLL

The ghost circled in red has 7 circles, blue hair and no red socks.

GHOULS AND GOBLINS

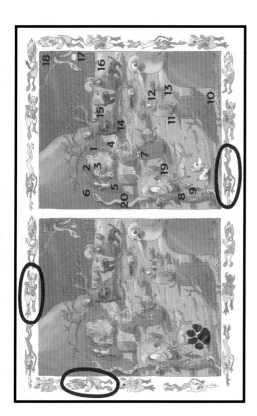

The 3 goblins circled all have purple ears, blue legs, 1 yellow glove and are not wearing pointy boots.

HAUNTED CASTLE

The portrait circled in red does not belong. (There is no black line on the fan.)

TRIP TO THE CEMETERY

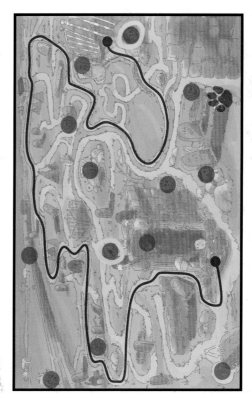

The 2 skeletons circled in yellow are pirates.

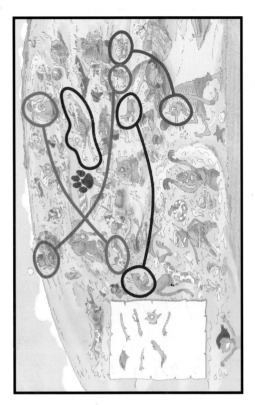

BOGEYMAN BEACH

The bogeymen all have belts and pointy ears. The bogeyman circled in red matches the bogey twin.

GHOST TOWN

The cowboy circled in blue is Bloody Bradley. 11 cowboys drink at the Sarsaparilla Saloon. 6 cowboys drink at the Horse Shine Hotel.

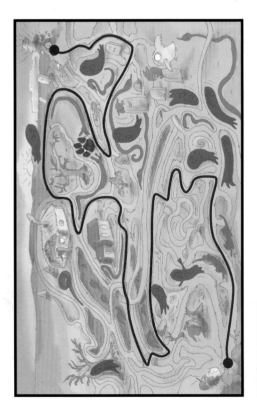

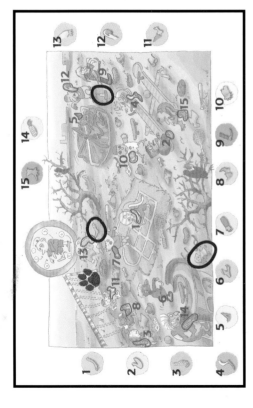

GHOSTCATCHERS

The ghost's lost glasses are circled in yellow. There are 4 goblins and 11 snakes.

ZOMBIE PLAYGROUND

The sock, the doll and the candle do not have a matching pair.